The Optimistic Heart

CJ FitzGerald

Presentation by *BookLeaf Publishing*

Web: www.bookleafpub.com

E-mail: info@bookleafpub.com

ISBN: 9789360947743

First edition 2024

ACKNOWLEDGEMENT

Thank you to my many friends, relatives, children and grandchildren for giving me many ideas for writing poetry and giving me encouragement to share it with the world. Special thanks to my Sister, Mary Lou Douglas, for helping me see the bright side of life, and being my biggest supporter.

PREFACE

CJ captures observations about human interactions, and as the eternal optimist, finds similarities in the subjects and characters she writes about. With empathy, and reverence she writes simply relatable poetry.

Our Hearts all Break and Find Joy the Same Way

There's an experience I had that I want to share
with you
It was in the past, couple decades ago, maybe a
few

It was very, very late – almost midnight
I arrived at Midway on a delayed flight

I had traveled alone, as I often did then
What time would I finally get home?
I didn't know when

I waited in silence with several others for the
Shuttle
Economy Lot passengers all in a scattered
huddle

No one spoke to each other, not a single word
All different people from all over the world

Certainly different nationalities, upbringings and
religious views
Just all of us standing there, looking down at our
shoes

The shuttle arrived and we all collapsed into our
seats
Still staring at nothing so we didn't have to
speak

Some music was playing on the shuttle radio
Even at this hour, the driver was a happy fellow

The song "My Girl" comes on and I couldn't
help myself
I started to sing along, very softly at first, until I
got help

The man next to me joined in, with a soulful
voice and louder
And wouldn't you know it, soon we were all
singing together!

The refrain starts – "I guess you say, what can
make me feel this way . . ."
A spontaneous joyful connection of strangers at
play

We're all laughing and singing - our very own
show
On an Economy Lot Shuttle in Chicago

We might have started our short journey
apprehensive for a while
Now we were all united by that universal
language
Music and a smile

We arrived at our stop just as the song finished,
and we parted ways
Our moment had passed, but I'll remember it
always

I said a little prayer for each of those passengers
that night
May they always feel safe, and may their hearts
always be light

I still think of them to this day, because that
moment changed my life
We're all on this shuttle together, and we should
live with less strife

There are more good people than bad in this
whole world
Our hearts all break the same way, and we
should put down the sword

This world belongs to Love and it's not ours to
fight about

It's amazing to me that we all can't figure this out

Open your heart and you'll see it beats just like mine
If we could all simply love, and not hate, we could all be fine

If we could all stop filling our minds with violent muses
From movies, TV, video games and even some music

I was raised in a broken home, but to me we were whole
We were taught to never hurt another soul

It's easy to be a victim of circumstance and decide to be cruel
Because in your life, bad things have happened to you

It takes guts to rise above this rage, as so many have
Stop acting entitled, and be brave enough to give

It seems when we all pray, our Gods are the same

I know mine would not ask me to kill in Their
name

You may call your God a different name than I
do
Whatever it is, I know they bring comfort to you

And if you don't agree with anything I say
I want to tell you that it's really okay

I won't hunt you down and hurt you if you
disagree
I will love you anyway, and your feelings should
be free

Many times it seems we've all been under attack
Let's keep hope alive and have each other's
backs

Pray for love and tolerance and hearts at ease
Most of all, pray for Peace

The Writing Man

So I was in Greek Town - this was the late '70s
I'm at this bar waiting for my first taste of Gyros
(I'm not sure I liked it)
Anyway I look across the bar
There's this intense man, writing hard and fast
on a yellow legal pad
He wore round, wire-rimmed glasses, his face
etched with a fierce expression
Jaw clenched
He's probably around 40, lanky yet muscular
His head was made of shaggy wayward, dull
blond curls that danced with every forceful
Stroke of his pen
He pressed so hard, you'd think he was going to
carve into the bar top
Shredding (like Prince's guitar)
He's writing furiously, maniacally
He wrote without a pause, a constant
Stream of Thought
With every dot of his "i", I felt like I was being
shoved hard with one finger
Like being provoked I sort of involuntarily
reeled back a bit
With every swift cross of his "t", I felt somehow
aroused

I understood him so we'll - the lyrics to "Killing
me Softly" going through my head (Roberta
Flack version)
Atavistic
He MUST write NOW
He's got to get it all said before he forgets
He MUST get it all on paper, and OUT of his
head
I was riveted watching him
I coveted his intensity
I wanted to somehow acknowledge our kinship,
but knew I never could
It's just not proper etiquette between writers to
interrupt
The Flow
I've been there myself -
I grappled for a surface to write on
A napkin, my hand
Anything!
Where's a pen!
It just seems genius at the time
More than anything, I wanted to read what he
wrote (I new I never would)
But it surely must have been about love or rage
Sometimes they look the same
After about 10 minutes, he stopped abruptly
He leaned back in his bar stool, and hooked one
arm over the back
Rested his pen against his lower lip

Gazed up at the ceiling and pondered
I knew what he was thinking - A better way to
phrase it
Editing is inevitable (it seriously never ends)
And so it commenced
With just as much ferociousness
Almost as if he were punishing himself
And so he was

An Old Friend

Sitting outside and enjoying a summer evening
A car speeds by, windows down, music blasting
It reminded me of an old friend
We were 19
Immortal
We were recklessly speeding south on Rt. 83
In his little MG convertible
It was late - around midnight
Our hair was flying around chaotic
Singing along to Springsteen's "Rosalita"
What a rush
We were laughing hard
It was thrilling
Oh the way he shifted gears
Hands so gifted - piano genius
He was tall, muscular and slim
Long blond hair
Light blue eyes
Robust laugh, but so soft spoken
We were very good friends
Sometimes, when I caught him looking at me
I felt adored and desired all at once
He became a composer - appropriate and perfect
Wherever he is now
I hope he's well and ridiculously happy

Hope

Her heart is racing but not from fear
From joy
Is she dreaming? She's not sure
Because it's all so vivid, so vibrant
She knows you can't see star tails with the naked
eye
But there they are!
Swirling, interwoven, dancing
On the background of a velvet navy sky
They look like God's love, like a Van Gogh
painting
They feel like the happy souls of every loving
mother have joined together
And they're pouring out peace, joy and
nurturing, blanketing the whole earth
Now she sees a cloud symphony
She opens her arms to embrace them
All their music
The world is a fesitval
Even if it is a dream, she knows all of this
happens every day
And she feels hope

Tears

11

The best part about a rainy summer night on the
front porch
Is that no one is walking by
It's just the sound of the rain as it hides my
falling tears

You are Loved

When you're struggling, remember
By your very nature
You are necessary
You were born into this world
Exactly
As planned and designed
You were born in your ultimate form
As natural as a sunrise
Express yourself as you wish
Love whomever your heart wants
You're here, so you are
Essential
When you think no one thinks of you
If you feel inconsequential
Remember the Universe loves you
We are all linked by human kindness
We are all the same *race*
Human
We are all *of* each other
From different parts of the Earth
Treat yourself with the
Reverence
You were created to
Deserve
Know this:
You are already a Divine masterpiece
You are loved

Life

Your life will consist of
Beginnings
And Endings
And Possibilities
And Tragedies
And Elation
And Opportunities
And Regrets
And Creativity
And Misunderstandings
And Mistakes
And Apologies
And Love
And Grief
The world is equally
Terrifying and magnificent
If you can manage the terrifying
It's far more magnificent
So go on with your bad self
Go live that life

Family Goals

Each year has it's new challenges
I never thought you'd be one of them
Let's start over today
I know better now
Do you?
Let's figure it out
I'm reaching out to you
Will you please reach back?

Comfort

15

To fit into the
Nook
Of someone's
Crannies
And cuddle
The best

Busy Mind

I have a chaotic, undisciplined mind
My mind is so damed busy
But I'm stuck doing nothing
Where to begin?
We all - at times - run our hands through our hair
And think to ourselves,
"I'm about to burst!"
It's imminent

First Love

You learn as you get older that your first love is
always part of your life
You will always remember the way you felt the
day you met
That instant mutual attraction
The laughter on carefree days together
The feeling of intimacy between souls
And you spend the rest of your life in search of
that feeling
And if you're lucky, you find that comfort again

To my Grandchildren

I am your Nana, and I love the sky
The sun and the moon and the clouds floating by
I love to gaze at the stars at night
Connecting our hearts with all my might
I will share all these wonders with you
Your whole family loves the sky too
You're made of stardust, and so am I
We were instantly woven in the blink of an eye
Before I even heard about you
You were a person I already knew
You've been in my dreams as long as I
remember
I am your Nana, and I'll love you forever

Clouds

19

I can't help myself when they come into view
I've gotta see what those clouds are about
I want to read their stories as they cruise on by
I love a good cloud symphony
And I want to dance inside all the shapes I see
I wonder where they're going
And can I go too?

The Vortex of Awesomeosity

Oh the love I have witnessed today
In this neighborhood
Friends and families walking together into town
Enjoying a roadie on the way
Parents walking home from the train and kids
running into their arms
Neighbors stopping by to chat for awhile
Our mail person, Lady Dee, gives a smile and
kind words
Music and laughter from backyards around us
Some young men playing guitars and trumpets
on their porch steps
A big brother helping his little brother learn to
ride his bike
Dogs romping up to each other while their
owners talk
Birds nesting in our tree
An older couple walking by hand in hand
Walkers rest on the bench built by my neighbor
The scent of bonfires and BBQ fill up the night
Our home is in a loving neighborhood
It's the happy VOA

Cosmic

What do we look like from celestial skies?
To the sun, moon and planets?
Do people on earth look like twinkling stars?
We're all made of star seed - we're each our own
galaxy
So maybe, when it's your birthday
You shine brighter than anyone else
Maybe the planets anticipate your extra glow
once a year
Like the meteor showers we await
Maybe we look like a sparkling galaxy of souls
at night
And the Cosmos looks at us in wonder too

The Eclipse

Oh the magnificence of today
Of the Earth
Of the Sun and Moon dancing
Of the Galaxy
Of the Universe
Of Love
Of Community
The world stands still to watch the wonder
Skies turn to sunset
Then to night
Bird songs stop and cricket songs start
Crescent shadows everywhere
Planets and constellations waving hello
Connection
Surrender
Peace

Happy Place

23

I'm wearing my Grandpa's Hawaiian shirt from
the '50's
It has coconut shell buttons
I'm sitting on the front porch swing alone on a
Saturday evening
While it rains
Listening to soul music
Am I the old lady sitting on her porch during a
rainstorm?
Indeed I am
And I feel peaceful

People

Each is unique
The best thing you can do is to let them
Be
Whomever they are
Just as you are
Love them as they be
With their quirks
With their mistakes
With their talents
Hell - if you look at yourself
You're a bit wackadoo too
I know I'm not everyone's favorite
Even if I wish I were
And I am grateful
For those who give me grace
And include me - even love me
Regardless
of my Wackadooness

One More Time

25

I'm thinking about a long kiss
And embrace
Not passion but
Mutual
Deep
Attraction
Adoration
Affection
True love
Comfort
Just one more time
In my lifetime
I long for this connection

Spring Drivers

Everyone driving by smiling with windows open
wide
Some cars have kids that are laughing and
waving hello
Some have music blasting
Some shout happy greetings
Some teens shout profanities
Some have dogs on their lap
Some people's hands are wind surfing out the
window
Hair flying free
And here I sit on the front porch swing
Watching so much love for the warm weather
Drive right by

Circles

Everything is at its most beautiful
at it's crescendo -
Just before it dies:
An ocean wave
A sunset
A sunrise
A starry night
Autumn leaves
Flowers
Our souls
Childhood
Innocence
A love story
A smile
A hearty laugh
A raindrop
A snowflake
A Thunderstorm
A bonfire
You get the drift
But they all begin again
And oh the joy in experiencing them over and
over

9 789360 947743